Exploring MOUNTAIN HABITATS with Big Bird

Charlotte Reed

Lerner Publications ◆ Minneapolis

There are many habitats to explore!

In the Sesame Street® Habitats series, young readers will take a tour of eight habitats. Join your friends from *Sesame Street* as they learn about these different habitats where animals live, sleep, and find food and water.

Sincerely,
The Editors at Sesame Workshop

Table of Contents

WHAT IS A HABITAT?

Let's explore habitats! A habitat is a place where animals live and can find water, food, and a place to sleep. A mountain habitat is a type of habitat.

Mountains are much taller than me!

Mountains can be very tall. The highest point of a mountain is called a peak or summit.

There are mountain habitats all over the world!

LET'S LOOK AT MOUNTAIN HABITATS

It's warmer at the bottom of the mountain. Full, green trees sometimes grow there. It's colder at the top of the mountain. Pine trees sometimes grow there.

To reach top of mountain, animals good climbers!

Mountain goats use their legs and hooves to help them climb up the mountains. Their hooves help them hold on to rocks.

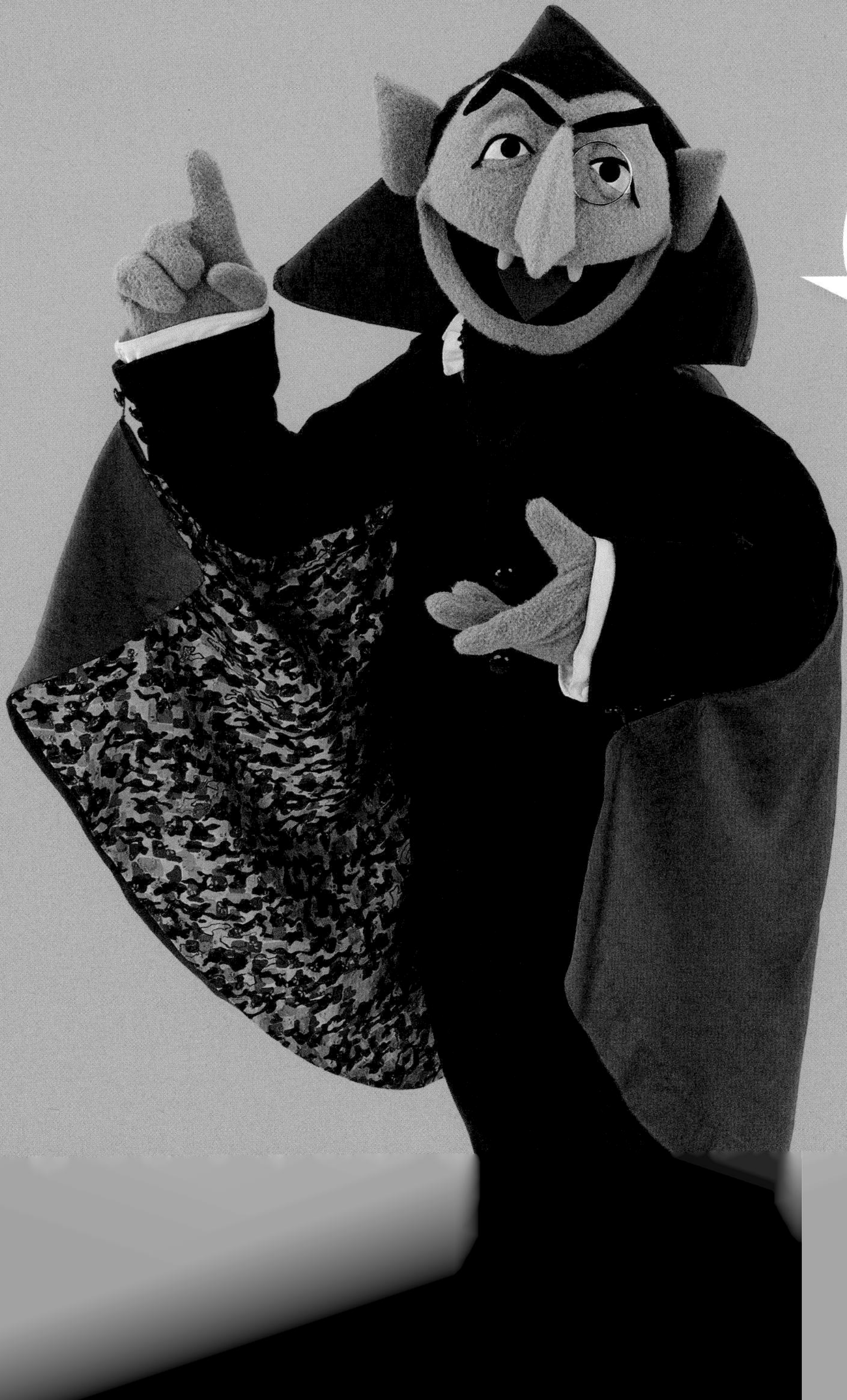

I see two! One, two
goats on the side
of the mountain.
Ah, ah, ah!

Golden eagles make their homes on mountains. Their nests are made of sticks, grass, and leaves. Golden eagles build their nests on the edge of a mountain or on a tree branch.

Golden eagles fly really fast!

Mountain lions live in the mountains too. They have strong legs that help them jump far and claws that help them climb trees.

That's a big cat!

Since it's colder at the top of the mountain, some animals, like elk, go to the bottom of the mountain during winter. The bottom is warmer.

A group of elk is called a herd.

The mountains where red pandas live are very cold. Red pandas have a thick fur coat that helps them stay warm.

Look at the red panda's long, fluffy tail!

This snowshoe hare also has warm fur to help it stay warm. Its white fur blends into the snow.

Help Elmo find the snowshoe hare!

In the winter months, ibexes grow hair under their fur to help them stay warm.

Yaks eat grass, herbs, and wild flowers. Their horns help them break through snow and ice so they can get to plants underneath.

Yaks live at the very top of the mountain!

Many animals make their home in mountain habitats. Which mountain animal do you want to learn more about?

I can't wait to learn more about them all!

CAN YOU GUESS?

1. Which of these pictures is of a mountain habitat?

A

B

2. Which of these animals lives in a mountain habitat?

A

B

Glossary

fur: the hairy coat on an animal

habitat: a place where animals live and can find water, food, and a place to sleep

hooves: hard coverings on the feet of some animals

summit: the highest point of a mountain

Can You Guess? Answers

1. B
2. A

Read More

Anthony, William. *Make a Mountain Range*. Minneapolis: Bearport, 2023.

Hicks, Dwayne. *That's a Mountain!* New York: Gareth Stevens, 2022.

Reed, Charlotte. *Explore Desert Habitats with Rosita*. Minneapolis: Lerner Publications, 2024.

Photo Acknowledgments

Image credits: Uwe-Bergwitz/iStock/Getty Images, p. 1; Gary Gray/iStock/Getty Images, p. 5; Lasting Image by Pedro Lastra/Moment/Getty Images, p. 6; Kjell Linder/Moment/Getty Images, p. 9; Jay Dickman/The Image Bank/Getty Images, p. 10; Ozbalci/iStock/Getty Images, p. 12; milehightraveler/E+/Getty Images, p. 14; Jaroslav Sugarek/iStock/Getty Images, p. 17; 1Tomm/iStock/Getty Images, p. 18; John Luke/Stockbyte/Getty Images, p. 21; Westend61/Getty Images, p. 22; Created by MaryAnne Nelson/Moment/Getty Images, p. 24; hadynyah/E+/Getty Images, p. 25; Sasha64f/iStock/Getty Images, p. 26; milehightraveler/iStock/Getty Images, p. 26 (circle); JamesBrey/E+/Getty Images, p. 27; bjeayes/iStock/Getty Images, p. 28 (A); Oleg Znamenskiy/Shutterstock, p. 28 (B); AscentXmedia/E+/Getty Images, p. 29 (A); Zoonar/Eugen Haag/Alamy, p. 29 (B).

Front cover: Kyle Kempf/iStock/Getty Images; Bkamprath/iStock/Getty Images (mountain goat).

Back cover: Jerry & Barb Jividen/Moment Open/Getty Images (snow leopard); falcon0125/Moment Open/Getty Images (ibex).

Index

For my mother, who taught me how to climb every mountain

Lerner Publications Company
An imprint of Lerner Publishing Group, Inc.
241 First Avenue North
Minneapolis, MN 55401 USA

For reading levels and more information, look up this title at www.lernerbooks.com.

Main body text set in Mikado provided by HVD.

Designer: Laura Otto Rinne **Photo Editor:** Annie Zheng
Lerner team: Martha Kranes

Library of Congress Cataloging-in-Publication Data

Names: Reed, Charlotte, 1997- author.
Title: Explore mountain habitats with Big bird / Charlotte Reed.
Description: Minneapolis : Lerner Publications, [2024] | Series: Sesame Street habitats | Includes bibliographical references and index. | Audience: Ages 4–8 | Audience: Grades K–1 | Summary: "Explore mountain habitats with Big Bird and the rest of your friends from Sesame Street. Young readers will discover different types of mountain habitats and the animals that live there"– Provided by publisher.
Identifiers: LCCN 2023007052 (print) | LCCN 2023007053 (ebook) | ISBN 9798765604243 (library binding) | ISBN 9798765617588 (epub)
Subjects: LCSH: Mountain animals—Habitations—Juvenile literature. | Mountain ecology—Juvenile literature. | BISAC: JUVENILE NONFICTION / Science & Nature / Environmental Science & Ecosystems
Classification: LCC QL113 .R44 2024 (print) | LCC QL113 (ebook) | DDC 591.75/3—dc23/eng/20230420

LC record available at https://lccn.loc.gov/2023007052
LC ebook record available at https://lccn.loc.gov/2023007053

ISBN 979-8-7656-2487-6 (pbk.)

Manufactured in the United States of America
1-1009561-51411-6/7/2023